GROW WITH ME

THE JOURNAL

OVERCOME CHALLENGES, EMBRACE AUTHENTICITY, AND CULTIVATE GROWTH

Dr. Lisa L Campbell®

A Note from Dr. Lisa L Campbell®

After writing my final chapter of "Grow with Me", I immediately realized that I needed to create a journal. As you read each chapter, I invite you to delve deeper into the transformative journey of personal growth, resilience, and self-discovery. For those who are not used to journaling, once you commit to it, you can experience moments of personal and professional growth. In my opinion, a journal is meant to be private and personal, but share parts of it, if you feel the need to. I write for therapy, I write to "Shed the Weight™" that I am carrying. Some may call it brain dumping, but no matter what you call it, you must get those thoughts good or bad out of your head!

SUMMARY OF "GROW WITH ME" BOOK CHAPTERS

Chapter 1: Life Challenges
In this opening chapter, "Life Challenges," I lay the foundation for the transformative journey that lies ahead. Life has a way of presenting us with obstacles and setbacks, but it is through these challenges that we find the strength to grow. I share my struggles and triumphs, offering you a glimpse into the power of perseverance, resilience, and determination.

Chapter 2: Education Journey
Education is a powerful tool that can unlock doors and open new opportunities. Just for context, the process of receiving an education is not just about attending college. When you are being educated no matter the format, you can experience growth! In this chapter, "Education Journey," I reflect upon the transformative power of learning and the impact it has had on my personal growth.

Chapter 3: Jasmine, a Deaf, Mute Child
In "Jasmine, a Deaf, Mute Child," I recount the heartwarming and profound story of navigating motherhood with my daughter, Jasmine. Her unique challenges as a deaf and mute individual have taught me valuable lessons about empathy, communication, and the importance of understanding one another.

Chapter 4: The House the Campbells Built

"The House the Campbells Built" is a metaphorical journey that explores the deeper meaning of family and spiritual growth. This chapter symbolizes the resilience and personal growth that can be achieved by facing challenges head-on. The Campbell's by their love and actions helped me realize that I was born with strength. You too have strength, but you must continue to grow to realize yours.

Chapter 5: You Work Too Much

In our fast-paced world, it is all too easy to become consumed by work and lose sight of what truly matters. In "You Work Too Much," I shed light on how others viewed my "work too much" mentality. This chapter is also where I explain my "why", everyone is not going to understand your vision, but if you create a plan, you owe it to "you" to execute it until the end. There will be challenges, but you can handle them by believing in yourself.

Chapter 6: They Don't Know Me or My Struggle

In this chapter, "They Don't Know Me or My Struggle," I confront the misconceptions, societal expectations, and the weight of judgment that I have encountered throughout my journey as a healthcare professional. I courageously embrace my authentic self and inspire you to do the same, recognizing that personal growth comes from staying true to oneself despite external pressures.

Chapter 7: Weight and the Wait

In "Weight and the Wait," I reflect upon the emotional burdens we carry, and the transformative power of learning go. Together, we will explore the process of shedding the weight that holds us back, allowing us to move forward on our personal growth journeys with renewed strength and clarity.

Chapter 8: The Village

No one achieves personal growth in isolation. In "The Village," I share stories of the positive impact of relationships and the role of a growth-oriented network. Together, we will discover the significance of a supportive community and the power of seeking connection, support, and inspiration from those who uplift and empower us.

Chapter 9: A Slaughter Woman

"A Slaughter Woman" delves into a defining moment of my journey where I embraced my role as a catalyst for personal growth. This chapter explores the transformative power of self-realization and the strength that comes from stepping into our purpose. If you continue to learn, growth will be the result, when the time is right!

Chapter 10: The Birth of the Growth Motivator

In this pivotal chapter, "The Birth of the Growth Motivator," I share the defining moment when I recognized my calling to empower individuals and foster community growth. Together, we will explore the transformative power of becoming catalysts for personal growth and inspiring others to embark on their journeys of self-discovery.

Chapter 11: The Growth Community

In "The Growth Community," I invite you into a world of like-minded individuals who are committed to personal growth and transformation. Together, we will explore the significance of creating a supportive community that nurtures our growth and provides a space for us to learn, share, and uplift one another.

Chapter 12: Faith over Fear

Faith has been an integral part of my journey, helping me overcome fear and find the strength to pursue personal growth. In this final chapter, "Faith over Fear," I reflect upon my faith development and the transformative power it holds in fostering resilience and personal growth. Faith is rooted in my believing in myself and consciously living out my dreams.

Conclusion

As you embark on this journey, I encourage you to reflect, engage, and explore the themes and lessons presented in each chapter. Use these pages as a space to delve into your own experiences, challenges, and aspirations, and discover the transformative power of personal growth. Together, let us embrace the path of growth and become the best versions of ourselves.

With warmest regards, Dr. Lisa L Campbell

Chapter 1

LIFE CHALLENGES

1. Reflect on a current challenge or obstacle you're facing in your life. How does it impact your overall well-being and progress toward your goals?

___
___
___
___
___
___
___
___
___
___
___
___
___
___
___
___
___
___
___
___
___
___
___
___
___
___

2. Describe a specific area of your life where you feel stuck or lacking motivation. What steps can you take to overcome this and move forward?

_____

_____

_____

_____

_____

_____

_____

_____

_____

_____

_____

_____

_____

_____

_____

_____

_____

_____

_____

_____

_____

_____

_____

3. Explore your aspirations and dreams. What are the biggest barriers holding you back from pursuing them, and how can you start addressing those barriers?

_____
_____
_____
_____
_____
_____
_____
_____
_____
_____
_____
_____
_____
_____
_____
_____
_____
_____
_____
_____
_____
_____
_____
_____
_____
_____

4. Consider your strengths and talents. How can you leverage them to overcome challenges and create positive change in your life?

_____
_____
_____
_____
_____
_____
_____
_____
_____
_____
_____
_____
_____
_____
_____
_____
_____
_____
_____
_____
_____
_____
_____

5. Imagine yourself successfully navigating through your current challenge and achieving your desired outcome. What does that look like, and how would it impact your life and happiness?

_____
_____
_____
_____
_____
_____
_____
_____
_____
_____
_____
_____
_____
_____
_____
_____
_____
_____
_____
_____
_____
_____
_____
_____

Chapter 2

EDUCATION JOURNEY

1. Consider the various ways you continue to learn and grow outside of traditional education. How have you sought knowledge and developed new skills through alternative means?

_____
_____
_____
_____
_____
_____
_____
_____
_____
_____
_____
_____
_____
_____
_____
_____
_____
_____
_____
_____
_____
_____
_____
_____

2. Explore the impact of personal responsibilities and growth. How have these experiences influenced your perspective on learning and self-development?

_____
_____
_____
_____
_____
_____
_____
_____
_____
_____
_____
_____
_____
_____
_____
_____
_____
_____
_____
_____
_____
_____
_____
_____
_____

3. Think about a significant moment or event during your journey of self-discovery that made you question your path or purpose. How did you navigate through this uncertainty, and what did you learn from the experience?

_____
_____
_____
_____
_____
_____
_____
_____
_____
_____
_____
_____
_____
_____
_____
_____
_____
_____
_____
_____
_____
_____
_____
_____
_____

4. Reflect on the different roles learning has played in uncovering your passions, values, and strengths. How has seeking knowledge and personal growth outside formal education helped shape your sense of identity and purpose?

_____
_____
_____
_____
_____
_____
_____
_____
_____
_____
_____
_____
_____
_____
_____
_____
_____
_____
_____
_____
_____
_____
_____
_____

5. Imagine yourself as a mentor or guide to someone facing similar struggles in their pursuit of knowledge and personal growth without formal education. What advice or insights would you offer to help them navigate their path, embrace self-discovery, and find fulfillment in their journey?

_____
_____
_____
_____
_____
_____
_____
_____
_____
_____
_____
_____
_____
_____
_____
_____
_____
_____
_____
_____
_____
_____

Chapter 3

JASMINE, A DEAF, MUTE CHILD

1. Reflect on a time in your life when you faced unexpected challenges that required you to grow up quickly and assume adult responsibilities. How did these experiences shape your perspective and personal growth?

_____
_____
_____
_____
_____
_____
_____
_____
_____
_____
_____
_____
_____
_____
_____
_____
_____
_____
_____
_____
_____
_____
_____
_____
_____
_____

2. Think about a time when you felt overwhelmed by the demands of adulthood or caregiving responsibilities. How did you navigate through those moments of uncertainty or self-doubt? What strategies or support systems helped you overcome challenges?

_____
_____
_____
_____
_____
_____
_____
_____
_____
_____
_____
_____
_____
_____
_____
_____
_____
_____
_____
_____
_____
_____
_____
_____

3. Reflect on growth and personal development that can come from facing adversity. How have these experiences shaped your identity and perspective on life? How have these experiences shaped your identity and perspective on life?

_____
_____
_____
_____
_____
_____
_____
_____
_____
_____
_____
_____
_____
_____
_____
_____
_____
_____
_____
_____
_____
_____
_____
_____
_____

4. Consider the importance of self-care and support networks for parents or caregivers. How have you prioritized your well-being while caring for others? What lessons can be learned from your experiences or those of others?

_____
_____
_____
_____
_____
_____
_____
_____
_____
_____
_____
_____
_____
_____
_____
_____
_____
_____
_____
_____
_____
_____
_____
_____
_____
_____

5. Imagine yourself providing guidance and support to an individual facing challenges. What advice or insights would you offer to help them navigate their journey of personal growth?

_____
_____
_____
_____
_____
_____
_____
_____
_____
_____
_____
_____
_____
_____
_____
_____
_____
_____
_____
_____
_____
_____

CHAPTER 4

THE HOUSE THE CAMPBELLS BUILT

1. Reflect on the role of older generations in your life and the strength they have imparted. How have their experiences and wisdom influenced your personal growth and resilience?

2. Describe a specific memory or moment when you felt empowered or inspired by the presence of an older family member or mentor. How did their guidance shape your confidence and outlook on life?

_____
_____
_____
_____
_____
_____
_____
_____
_____
_____
_____
_____
_____
_____
_____
_____
_____
_____
_____
_____
_____
_____
_____
_____
_____
_____
_____

3. Explore the qualities and values you have learned from influential leaders or mentors outside of your family. How have their leadership and support impacted your personal growth and development?

_____
_____
_____
_____
_____
_____
_____
_____
_____
_____
_____
_____
_____
_____
_____
_____
_____
_____
_____
_____
_____
_____
_____
_____
_____

4. Reflect on a time when you faced a significant challenge or obstacle and drew strength from the teachings or guidance of an influential leader. How did their words or actions help you navigate the situation and grow as an individual?

_____
_____
_____
_____
_____
_____
_____
_____
_____
_____
_____
_____
_____
_____
_____
_____
_____
_____
_____
_____
_____
_____
_____
_____

5. Reflect on how you have been able to inspire and uplift others through your actions and leadership. How has this experience influenced your own self-confidence and personal growth?

Chapter 5

YOU WORK TOO MUCH

1. Reflect on your work-life balance. How do you prioritize rest, self-care, and leisure activities amidst your professional commitments? How does this balance contribute to your overall well-being and fulfillment?

_____
_____
_____
_____
_____
_____
_____
_____
_____
_____
_____
_____
_____
_____
_____
_____
_____
_____
_____
_____
_____
_____
_____
_____
_____

2. Describe a specific self-care practice or activity that helps you recharge and maintain a healthy mindset. How does incorporating self-care into your routine positively impact your productivity and motivation?

3. Explore the concept of purpose in your work. What gives your work meaning and a sense of fulfillment? How does having a clear purpose influence your motivation and approach to your professional life?

_____
_____
_____
_____
_____
_____
_____
_____
_____
_____
_____
_____
_____
_____
_____
_____
_____
_____
_____
_____
_____
_____
_____
_____
_____

4. Consider the benefits of setting boundaries and establishing a healthy work-life integration. How have you found ways to disconnect from work and prioritize personal time? Share strategies that have helped you maintain a healthy balance.

___
___
___
___
___
___
___
___
___
___
___
___
___
___
___
___
___
___
___
___
___
___
___
___
___
___
___

5. Explore the connection between your values and your professional pursuits. How does aligning your work with your core values contribute to your sense of purpose and fulfillment? Share examples of how your work reflects your values.

_____
_____
_____
_____
_____
_____
_____
_____
_____
_____
_____
_____
_____
_____
_____
_____
_____
_____
_____
_____
_____
_____
_____

CHAPTER 6

THEY DON'T KNOW ME OR MY STRUGGLE

1. Reflect on a time when you felt judged or misunderstood by others. How did this impact your sense of self and personal growth? How did you navigate through these judgments?

___

2. Explore the importance of self-acceptance and staying true to your journey despite external judgments. How have you cultivated resilience and confidence in the face of criticism or misunderstanding?

___
___
___
___
___
___
___
___
___
___
___
___
___
___
___
___
___
___
___
___
___
___
___
___
___
___

3. Reflect on the power of empathy and understanding in breaking down barriers of judgment. How have you learned to empathize with others and suspend judgment yourself? Share a specific example of when this understanding made a difference.

_____
_____
_____
_____
_____
_____
_____
_____
_____
_____
_____
_____
_____
_____
_____
_____
_____
_____
_____
_____
_____
_____
_____
_____
_____
_____
_____
_____
_____

4. Reflect on the role of self-belief and inner strength in overcoming external judgments. How have you found the courage to pursue your path despite criticism or doubt from others?

___
___
___
___
___
___
___
___
___
___
___
___
___
___
___
___
___
___
___
___
___
___
___
___
___

5. Imagine yourself as a source of inspiration for others who may be facing judgment or misunderstandings. How can you share your experiences and insights to encourage empathy, understanding, and growth in those around you?

CHAPTER 7

WEIGHT AND THE WAIT

1. Reflect on your relationship with your body and weight. How have society's standards and expectations influenced your perception of self? How has this impacted your overall well-being?

_____
_____
_____
_____
_____
_____
_____
_____
_____
_____
_____
_____
_____
_____
_____
_____
_____
_____
_____
_____
_____
_____
_____
_____
_____
_____

2. Describe a time when you felt pressured to conform to certain body ideals. How did this affect your self-esteem and self-worth? How have you worked towards embracing your body as it is?

_____
_____
_____
_____
_____
_____
_____
_____
_____
_____
_____
_____
_____
_____
_____
_____
_____
_____
_____
_____
_____
_____
_____
_____
_____

3. Explore the concept of waiting for a change in weight and body image. How do you navigate the balance between acceptance and desiring positive transformation? How do you practice patience and self-compassion in this journey?

4. Reflect on the impact of social media on body image and self-perception. How have you managed to maintain a healthy perspective while being exposed to these influences? What strategies have helped you foster a positive body image?

___
___
___
___
___
___
___
___
___
___
___
___
___
___
___
___
___
___
___
___
___
___
___
___
___
___
___

5. Consider the broader definition of "weight" beyond physical weight, such as emotional weight or societal expectations. How have you dealt with these different forms of weight in your life? How have you lightened your emotional load?

_____
_____
_____
_____
_____
_____
_____
_____
_____
_____
_____
_____
_____
_____
_____
_____
_____
_____
_____
_____
_____
_____
_____
_____

Chapter 8

THE VILLAGE

1. Reflect on the role of your support system in your life. How have your family and/or friends played a significant role in providing support, encouragement, and guidance during challenging times?

_____
_____
_____
_____
_____
_____
_____
_____
_____
_____
_____
_____
_____
_____
_____
_____
_____
_____
_____
_____
_____
_____
_____
_____
_____

2. Describe a specific moment when your friends played a crucial role in your personal growth and well-being. How did their presence and support contribute to your resilience and ability to overcome obstacles?

_____
_____
_____
_____
_____
_____
_____
_____
_____
_____
_____
_____
_____
_____
_____
_____
_____
_____
_____
_____
_____
_____
_____
_____
_____
_____

3. Reflect on the qualities of your closest friends that make them a strong part of your support system. How have they shown up for you during difficult moments? How do you reciprocate their support?

_____
_____
_____
_____
_____
_____
_____
_____
_____
_____
_____
_____
_____
_____
_____
_____
_____
_____
_____
_____
_____
_____
_____

4. Consider the importance of nurturing and maintaining relationships within your support system. How do you prioritize and invest in these relationships? How has this contributed to your overall sense of belonging and well-being?

_____
_____
_____
_____
_____
_____
_____
_____
_____
_____
_____
_____
_____
_____
_____
_____
_____
_____
_____
_____
_____
_____
_____
_____

5. Reflect on the concept of chosen family or close friends who have become like family to you. How have these relationships provided a sense of belonging and stability in your life? How do you cultivate and strengthen these connections?

_____
_____
_____
_____
_____
_____
_____
_____
_____
_____
_____
_____
_____
_____
_____
_____
_____
_____
_____
_____
_____
_____
_____
_____

Chapter 9:

A SLAUGHTER WOMAN

1. Describe a situation where you confidently spoke your mind and stood up for what you believed in. How did this experience impact your sense of self and personal growth? How did it affect your relationships or the outcomes of the situation?

_____
_____
_____
_____
_____
_____
_____
_____
_____
_____
_____
_____
_____
_____
_____
_____
_____
_____
_____
_____
_____
_____
_____
_____
_____

2. Explore the connection between physical strength and mental fortitude. How have you experienced the interplay between physical and mental strength in your own life? How do they support and reinforce each other?

_____
_____
_____
_____
_____
_____
_____
_____
_____
_____
_____
_____
_____
_____
_____
_____
_____
_____
_____
_____
_____
_____
_____
_____
_____

3. Reflect on the importance of authenticity and integrity in being a person who means what they say. How have you aligned your words and actions to create congruence in your life? How has this contributed to your sense of empowerment?

_____
_____
_____
_____
_____
_____
_____
_____
_____
_____
_____
_____
_____
_____
_____
_____
_____
_____
_____
_____
_____
_____
_____
_____
_____
_____

4. Consider the impact of positive self-talk and affrmations on cultivating a strong mindset. How have you used self-talk to overcome challenges and reinforce your belief in yourself? Share specific examples and their effects.

___
___
___
___
___
___
___
___
___
___
___
___
___
___
___
___
___
___
___
___
___
___
___

5. Reflect on the symbolic significance of the Slaughter Woman in your own life. How does her image inspire and empower you? How can you embody her qualities of strength, resilience, and determination in your journey?

_____
_____
_____
_____
_____
_____
_____
_____
_____
_____
_____
_____
_____
_____
_____
_____
_____
_____
_____
_____
_____
_____
_____
_____
_____

Chapter 10

THE BIRTH OF THE GROWTH MOTIVATOR

1. Reflect on a time when you experienced personal growth and how it positively impacted your life. How did this experience inspire you to seek further growth and development?

2. Consider a specific area in your life where you feel motivated to make positive changes and achieve new levels of success. What steps can you take to embrace a growth mindset and overcome challenges in that area?

_____
_____
_____
_____
_____
_____
_____
_____
_____
_____
_____
_____
_____
_____
_____
_____
_____
_____
_____
_____
_____
_____
_____
_____
_____

3. Explore your goals and aspirations. What specific outcomes do you hope to achieve in your personal or professional life? How can adopting a growth mindset and accessing external resources support your journey toward those goals?

_____
_____
_____
_____
_____
_____
_____
_____
_____
_____
_____
_____
_____
_____
_____
_____
_____
_____
_____
_____
_____
_____
_____
_____
_____
_____

4. Reflect on the power of community and the support of like-minded individuals in your growth journey. How can engaging with programs and workshops that foster a growth mindset provide you with the necessary support and accountability?

_____
_____
_____
_____
_____
_____
_____
_____
_____
_____
_____
_____
_____
_____
_____
_____
_____
_____
_____
_____
_____
_____
_____
_____

5. Imagine the possibilities that could arise from developing a growth mindset and actively pursuing personal development. How could this positively impact your relationships, career, and overall well-being?

___
___
___
___
___
___
___
___
___
___
___
___
___
___
___
___
___
___
___
___
___
___
___

CHAPTER 11

THE GROWTH COMMUNITY

1. Reflect on a time when you felt supported and uplifted by being part of a community. How did this experience positively impact your personal growth and well-being?

_____
_____
_____
_____
_____
_____
_____
_____
_____
_____
_____
_____
_____
_____
_____
_____
_____
_____
_____
_____
_____
_____
_____
_____
_____

2. Explore the benefits of being surrounded by like-minded individuals who share similar goals and values. How can a community provide valuable resources, encouragement, and a sense of belonging on your growth journey?

_____
_____
_____
_____
_____
_____
_____
_____
_____
_____
_____
_____
_____
_____
_____
_____
_____
_____
_____
_____
_____
_____
_____
_____
_____

3. Consider the power of collective knowledge and shared experiences within a community. How can learning from others' insights and perspectives accelerate your growth and provide new development opportunities?

___

4. Imagine the possibilities for collaboration and networking within a community. How can connecting with others who share your interests and aspirations lead to new partnerships, mentorship opportunities, and personal growth?

_____
_____
_____
_____
_____
_____
_____
_____
_____
_____
_____
_____
_____
_____
_____
_____
_____
_____
_____
_____
_____
_____
_____
_____
_____

5. Reflect on the diverse perspectives and backgrounds that can be found within a community. How can exposure to different ideas and experiences broaden your understanding and foster personal growth?

CHAPTER 12

FAITH OVER FEAR

1. Reflect on a specific fear or limiting belief that has held you back from pursuing your true potential. How has this fear impacted your life, and what steps can you take to shift from fear to faith to step into your destiny?

_____
_____
_____
_____
_____
_____
_____
_____
_____
_____
_____
_____
_____
_____
_____
_____
_____
_____
_____
_____
_____
_____

2. Describe a time when you faced a significant challenge or obstacle and summoned the courage to overcome it through faith. How did this experience empower you and open doors to new possibilities?

___

3. Reflect on the impact of shifting your mindset from limitation to possibility. How can reframing your fears as opportunities for growth and transformation propel you forward in stepping into your destiny?

_____
_____
_____
_____
_____
_____
_____
_____
_____
_____
_____
_____
_____
_____
_____
_____
_____
_____
_____
_____
_____
_____
_____
_____
_____

4. Consider the role of self-belief and trust in the process of stepping into your destiny. How can cultivating unwavering faith in your abilities and purpose help you overcome self-doubt and seize opportunities that align with your true calling?

_____
_____
_____
_____
_____
_____
_____
_____
_____
_____
_____
_____
_____
_____
_____
_____
_____
_____
_____
_____
_____
_____
_____

5. Imagine yourself fully embracing your destiny and living a life driven by faith rather than fear. What steps can you take today to align your thoughts, choices, and actions with this vision? How will stepping into your destiny impact your sense of fulfillment and overall well-being?

_____
_____
_____
_____
_____
_____
_____
_____
_____
_____
_____
_____
_____
_____
_____
_____
_____
_____
_____
_____
_____
_____
_____
_____
_____

ONE FINAL NOTE FROM DR. LISA L CAMPBELL®

Are you ready to embark on a transformative growth journey, unlocking your true potential and embracing a life filled with purpose and fulfillment? I hope you have enjoyed the "Grow with Me" Journey, which is a powerful tool designed to guide you through self-reflection, inspiration, and personal development.

The growth journey doesn't end within the pages of this journal. I invite you to connect with me and become part of "The Growth Community." By joining our community, you will gain access to exclusive workshops, coaching programs, and a network of like-minded individuals dedicated to personal growth and continuous learning. Together, we will provide the support, guidance, and accountability you need to flourish on your journey.

Are you ready to "Grow Together"? Visit our website to schedule a complimentary consultation: **https://thegrowthmotivator.com**

www.ingramcontent.com/pod-product-compliance
Lightning Source LLC
LaVergne TN
LVHW061600070526
838199LV00077B/7122